Drawing Near

An Invitation to Prayer

Michael Fargo

TO THE MONKS OF
MT. ANGEL ABBEY

*Your very presence is a witness
that prayer is a way of life.*

CONTENTS

ACKNOWLEDGMENTS

The contents of this book began as a class I taught many years ago at Trinity Covenant Church in Salem, Oregon. The many thoughtful responses by participants have contributed greatly to my understanding. To my wife, Joy, I owe thanks for her faithful editing.

Scripture quotations (unless indicated otherwise) are taken from the New International Version (1984), Zondervan Publishing House, Grand Rapids, Michigan.

Preface

My soul thirsts for God, for the living God.
When can I go and meet with God?
Psalm 42:2

಄৹ஃ

There is something ironic about this book and *every* book ever written on prayer. It's an irony that we all know personally. It's both what caused some to pick this book up, as well as what kept others from even touching it. And the irony is this: we all instinctively know that prayer is one of the primary ways we connect to God, and therefore something that should be deeply meaningful. And yet far too often it isn't. In fact, a lot of the time prayer seems less than meaningful and even difficult. In short, we *all* struggle with it. The literature on prayer is immense, and a great deal of it begins with a confession of just how hard prayer can be.

I recently read two books on prayer by highly respected Christian leaders—Timothy Keller, former pastor of one of the largest churches in New York City, and J. I. Packer, for many years a professor of theology at Regent College in Canada. In both of their books they candidly share what a struggle prayer has been for much of their adult life. Another well-known theologian, Donald Bloesch, wrote an entire book entitled *The Struggle of Prayer*.

So obviously, if prayer is difficult for you, you're in good company. But there is also some hopeful news. These same people also describe how they have *grown* in prayer, and how, over time, it has truly become their lifeline to God. This is certainly my story; I would be lost without prayer. It has kept my faith from becoming a stale abstraction and shaping it into a living reality.

So if this little book helps you grow in that same direction, *even a little*, then it will have been worth all our time.

I would like to focus on three main areas:

- What is prayer and why do we pray?
- What did Jesus teach and model about prayer?
- How can we grow in prayer, both individually and corporately?

There are many wonderful books in print on this subject (as well as some really bad ones). Prayer is truly a vast topic, with many different aspects to it that I do not touch on at all. I am simply trying to help people *begin* the journey of engaging in prayer in a way that is personal, meaningful, and practical. And it's only by starting a journey that we can ever hope to get anywhere.

Chapter 1

What is Prayer?

Listen to my prayer, O God,
Do not ignore my plea; hear me and answer me.
My thoughts trouble me and I am distraught...
Psalm 55:1-2

ॐॐ

What is prayer? A ritual? A liturgy? A spiritual discipline we practice because it's supposed to be good for us (like taking vitamins)? Is it a "chat" with God or a mystical encounter? Does it need to be an emotional moment or does a quiet meditation qualify? Some folks claim prayer is all of the above and more, which may be true in one sense, but that's partly what makes prayer so difficult to understand. Perhaps it would be better to begin at a more basic level.

Where did our word "prayer" come from? Our English word comes from the Latin root *pecare*, which in French became *priere*, and through the Norman

Conquest it finally came into English. In Latin and French, it meant "to obtain something by entreaty." And this is undoubtedly what most people think of when they think of prayer—going to God with our needs. And in fact, most of the prayers in the Bible, and especially in the Psalms, are entreaties to God.

In the New Testament there are primarily three words that are translated 'prayer' from the underlying Greek:

- εὐχομαι—to desire something (and it's usually translated as "wish" rather than prayer, such as when Paul said: "*I could wish that I were accursed for the sake of my fellow Jews*"). Only twice in scripture is it usually translated as prayer.

- προσευχομαι—notice the preposition "προσ" (which means "to, toward, or with") is affixed to εὐχομαι, thus indicating that our desire is now directed *at* or *to* someone. This is the most common word for prayer in the New Testament, since Christian prayer is not an idle wish, but a desire directed to God.

- δεομαι—this means "to entreat or beseech someone earnestly," and is closer to the Latin *pecare*.

So obviously, at its core prayer involves our coming to God with a desire for something. Now I realize that many of the prayers people offer to God involve praise, worship, thanksgiving, confession, intersession, and so forth, and we will discuss these aspects of prayer later. But even these are still entreaties of a sort. When Jesus gives us the "Lord's Prayer," it sounds like it opens in praise ("*Our Father, who art in heaven, hallowed be thy name")*. Yet the opening verb is actually not in the subjunctive but the imperative mood—*'let your name be hallowed.'* We are asking God that his name be treated as it ought to be, both in us and in the world: In short, *we are asking for something.*

This raises the question: What sorts of things ought we to pray for? The short answer is anything and everything! Yes, in the Lord's Prayer, Jesus taught us to pray for the coming of God's kingdom, but he also mentions our daily bread, the forgiveness of our sins and help in temptation. The prayers in the Psalms cover virtually all dimensions of human existence and need. Nothing is off limits, nothing too trivial or controversial, nothing that God doesn't want us to include.

Which raises yet another question: Do we only pray to God for things that we can't secure for ourselves? No. When Jesus' taught us to pray for our daily bread, he still expected us to go out and work for it. Most of the things we pray for are still things which require *some* level of effort on our part. We shouldn't expect things to just fall out of the sky. What's more, there are many, many things we pray for which atheists don't pray for, and yet they still receive them.

So, then, why do we bother to pray for things at all? And right here we begin to inch closer to what genuine prayer is all about. There is a wonderful insight in Psalm 127 that reads, *"Unless the Lord builds the house, the builders labor in vain. Unless the Lord watches over the city, the guards stand watch in vain."* In other words, we don't pray to align God with what is going on in our lives, but we pray to align ourselves with what God

7

is already doing. We pray for specific things not to remind God of what he isn't already aware of (and concerned about), but to share with him what is going on inside of us, what presently concerns us and troubles us (or causes us to rejoice). We pray to *God* because we have no other place to go, no other resource that can truly address our deepest needs.

The more we grow in our understanding of God (and consequently, of reality), the more aware we become of something Paul said in his sermon to the citizens of Athens: *"He* [God] *gives us life and breath and everything else."* And then later he adds: *"In him we live and move and have our being."* In other words, Christians should be intimately aware that every breath we take, every beat of our heart, even our ability to think and reason, is a direct and *continual* gift from God. Those who do not know God assume these things all function according to some immutable, natural law. But Christians know better—or at least they should. All life is a continual gift from God and *as such it can be taken away at any time.*

It's the parable of the rich farmer all over again (Luke 12:13-21). He thought his own skill had achieved his wealth for him, and therefore he thought he could do with it as he pleased. Then, as Jesus put it, *"But God said to him, 'You fool! This very night your life will be demanded from you. Then who will get what you have prepared for yourself?'"* Jesus' point is that *all* of life— every moment of every day—is in the hands of God, and thus we ought never take anything for granted, but live continuously in the knowledge that it is *God* who sustains us. And this reality will certainly shape how we pray.

But even this is still too narrow an understanding of prayer. There are other reasons we pray besides our personal needs. We often pray to simply *thank* God for his provision and help, especially after we have been through some deep waters. We often pray to confess our sins and to seek God's forgiveness and restoration. We pray on behalf of others, especially those we love. These are all very important and common uses of prayer.

But there is something, especially in the prayers of Jesus and in many of the psalms, that do not involve any of these things. At its most mature level, we pray *to simply be with God,* to be in his presence, to enjoy him, to listen for what he might have to say to us, or to simply reflect on God *in himself* while we are consciously with him. At its most meaningful level, prayer is a way to simply be with God and to discover the joy and peace that fellowship with him offers.

But if the word prayer, in both English and in the New Testament, primarily means to seek something from God, why is this kind of prayer—merely being with God—even called prayer at all? Because, quite simply, our greatest *need* is not food, clothing, shelter, creative pursuits, or even human companionship. Our greatest need is *God himself.* To both know and be known by him. To love and be loved by him. Since he is the source of all beauty, truth, love, and meaning, these things can only retain their potency in connection with him. Apart from him our perception of beauty, truth, and love always goes bad.

Yes, God has given us this material world as a place to live, enjoy, and nurture. Yes, he's given us our family, friends, work, creative pursuits, and so forth, to help us experience a meaningful life. But apart from God, they all become fragile and illusive in the end. Loved ones can disappoint us, even betray us. Creativity can wane, common human pleasures can become tepid or even lose all value. Life without God reduces everything to a one-dimensional and primarily material existence. Deep meaning, deep satisfaction comes when we remain connected to the transcendent reality of God himself.

God obviously knows us and loves us even when we don't care about him. As Jesus put it, he still makes the sun shine on both good and bad people. But when we are strangers to his love, we don't benefit from it. I know and love my kids a lot, but there have been seasons (especially when they were teenagers) when they wanted very little to do with me, and thus our relationship became somewhat distant. I still knew and loved them a lot, and in ways they didn't always realize I continued to care for them. But there wasn't as much warmth or mutual sharing. And when this happens in our relationship to God, we lose access to the One who is the source of life at its deepest level.

But there is also an irony in all this. Do only religious people pray? I have observed that even people who have no conscious faith in God still engage in a kind of prayer. Most of us have been in crowds when disasters have happened—car wreck, fire, sudden sickness. It's amazing how often the people who profess no faith at all will suddenly say things like, "God help us," or "God have mercy," and so forth. Now there are lots of reasons why people talk like this, and many of the reasons have nothing to do with genuine faith at all. Such talk can be an emotional, cultural, knee-jerk reaction. But that doesn't matter, because my primary question right now is whether such talk still qualifies as a prayer.

What we discover is that even a plea to the "great whatever" is heard by God. In my twenties I was a radical unbeliever and yet there was a moment when I was in great despair and audibly called out "help!" I wasn't praying to anyone. I wasn't conscious of reaching out to some kind of "higher power." I was simply overwhelmed by a sense of drowning in the vast ocean of meaninglessness that my life had become. In fact, the ocean was so vast that I felt convinced no one could hear me, yet I felt compelled to call out just the same. And in a very dramatic way help came, and came quickly.

We see a similar thing happen in the New Testament (from Luke 5:1-11):

> One day as Jesus was standing by the Lake of Gennesaret, the people were crowding around him and listening to the word of God. He saw at the water's edge two boats, left there by the fishermen, who were washing their nets. He got into one of the boats, the one belonging to Simon, and asked him to put out a little from shore. Then he sat down and taught the people from the boat. When he had finished speaking, he said to Simon, "Put out into deep water, and let down the nets for a catch." Simon answered, "Master, we've worked hard all night and haven't caught anything. But because you say so, I will let down the nets." When they had done so, they caught such a large number of fish that their nets began to break. So they signaled their partners in the other boat to come and help them, and they came and filled

11

both boats so full that they began to sink. When Simon Peter saw this, he fell at Jesus' knees and said, "Go away from me, Lord; I am a sinful man!" For he and all his companions were astonished at the catch of fish they had taken, and so were James and John, the sons of Zebedee, Simon's partners. Then Jesus said to Simon, "Don't be afraid; from now on you will fish for people."

Now has Peter just prayed to Jesus? Observe the details. Peter is confronted by the sudden reality that Jesus is no regular person. Peter falls to his knees (which certainly looks like prayer), and entreats him to do something (specifically, to go away), as well as to confessing his own sinfulness. Has Peter just prayed to Jesus? *Yes, he has.* Peter may not think he is praying in the technical, religious sense of the word, but he is. It may not feel like the ancient prayers he is used to saying as an observant Jew. But in terms of what God hears, Peter has prayed and prayed well, for quickly Jesus answers, "Don't be afraid; from now on you will catch men." Jesus denies Peter his *literal* request (that Jesus would go away), but begins to answer his underlying need (to be forgiven his sins and given a purpose in his life). As we will discover, God answers all our prayers this way. He doesn't simply give us what we ask for, but what we actually need.

Do we often pray like this, not realizing that we are actually praying? Yes, we do—and we do it a lot. Especially in our interior lives—our thoughts, fears, empathy, longings—we are sending up prayers to God often. But if prayer, in one sense, is so ordinary, natural, and even unconscious, why is it also such a struggle for most people? In reflecting on this question for many years, I have observed at least some of the following at play (realizing, of course, that there are likely many other reasons too):

- *Unrealistic expectations*: we often carry around an image of prayer that has nothing to do with reality. We make it into something so lofty, profound, moving, articulate, or supernatural, that our actual prayers feel empty, flat, disconnected from anything real—just words spoken into the air with no one listening.

- *Unspoken needs*: we fail to be utterly transparent in our prayers and adopt a spiritual persona that is basically false. For prayer to be real, *we* have to be real, and that means bringing our real self to God.

- *Distractions*: we live in a busy, noisy, distracting world that is always competing for our attention. Until we are ruthless about creating space for prayer—and that means time, silence, and a non-distracting space—our prayers will continually be thwarted by both interior and exterior interruptions.

- *Unbelief*: it's very hard to grow in prayer if we are not also growing in our overall faith in God. To come to prayer with unaddressed doubts is to have our prayers continually undermined. One can certainly experience authentic prayer while struggling with doubt, but only if that same doubt is brought *into* our prayers, laid before God, and eventually brought to some level of resolution. Too many people today make a virtue out of chronic doubt, or they at least make it a badge of spirituality. Consequently, they are often people who remain frustrated in their prayers.

- *Bad theology*: this will be a topic throughout this book. There is a whole lot of false theology about God, reality, and prayer itself that makes learning how to pray very difficult.
- *Laziness*: like virtually everything meaningful in life, prayer takes time, energy, and effort. If we resist discipline of any kind, we will have a very difficult time growing in prayer.
- *Sin*: Many, many times in scripture God declares, "Stop praying! You're not dealing with your sin, so I refuse to hear you," such as we read in the opening verses of Isaiah 59. Jesus in the *Sermon on the Mount* warns us that if we want to bring something to God, and "your brother has something against you, leave your offering and first be reconciled with your brother." Or as Peter tells husbands in his first epistle (3:7), they should treat their wives well, "so that nothing will hinder your prayers." Yes, if we are caught in a sin and struggling with it, God certainly wants us to bring it to him in prayer as a means of confession and restoration. But if we are nurturing that sin, justifying it or holding on to it, then all our prayers are futile.

So what's my point in all this? *All* humans (both secular and religious) pray, and pray more often than we think. Our prayers rise up from deep within us. The cause of our prayer may not feel spiritual at all. The prayer may be prompted just as easily by very positive experiences as well as negative ones. It might be provoked by watching the birth a baby or giving a daughter away in marriage. Often the prayer is a natural reaction to very ordinary circumstances. Have you noticed how often a simple walk in the woods can generate an involuntary "thank you" to God from deep inside?

But if that is all prayer is, if it simply ends there, it can become a stillborn prayer that never goes anywhere, never consciously connects with the rest of what we know and believe. At best it remains a very infantile prayer to "the great whatever." But *Christian* prayer is born when it's knowingly directed at the God revealed in Christ—our Creator, Redeemer, Master, and Father. It's discovering that God is not some cosmic force or ideal. For want of a better term, we are forced to use the word Person in describing God— even though he's not merely one person among many persons, but *the* Person who makes human personality even possible. Prayer is the *means* by which we learn how to relate to God properly.

But if prayer is one of the key means for developing a relationship with God, then what are some of the core elements of any good relationship between "persons"? Think of your very best human relationships, and then ask yourself: What characterizes them all? At a minimum, I would suggest you would find the following:

- *Trust:* how can we share honestly with someone that we really don't trust? Trust in the New Testament is usually translated "faith." Prayer grows as we grow in our trust toward God.
- *Love:* those we love the most we want to be with the most. I use the word here not in the romantic or sentimental sense, but in the Christian sense of valuing the other more than myself—of laying

15

down my life for the other, even if that happens though countless mundane acts of caring. To love like this means we want to be with that other person. And what is the greatest command according to Jesus? "To love God with all our heart, soul, mind, and strength."

- *Communication*: what happens to human relationships—take marriage, for example—when people stop talking to one another? It dies! If we truly long to know, love, and be with God, we will pray. And our prayers will be more than a mere litany of formalities, but the deep, genuine sharing of our hearts—in praise, petition, and listening.

- *Time and energy*: I loved my wife a lot when I married her, but I love her a whole lot more now and for a whole bunch of different reasons. We have been though many things together and our trust has grown, and our ability to communicate has grown. This did not happen overnight. In fact, it took many, many years before I even began to feel like I really knew what I was doing. I didn't know how to share myself at first. I was often misunderstood by my wife, because she didn't really understand me. I can't stress enough to those who are married under 15 years, that the best is yet to come—that you still have a great many things to learn as well as unlearn. Be patient. Be in it for the long haul. Do you see how prayer is the same?

In short, prayer makes everything about our faith real. Theology can easily become an abstraction. Obedience can be a mere gesture, a "doing the right thing for all the wrong reasons." Religious observances (including song, liturgy and sacrament) can remain merely that—pious observances. And even our prayers can be one of those pious observances.

But true prayer, that authentic response of the real, inner me to the known reality of God, can transform everything. Even the most mundane, everyday dimensions of life are transformed as they become infused with the presence of God. To transparently allow the real me to sit before the real God, and then to articulate what I am really thinking and feeling, is to discover who *we* are and who *God* is as he reveals himself to us. I love the way Jesus puts it in John 14:21-23 during the last supper:

> *He who loves me will be loved by my Father, and I too will love him and disclose myself to him. ...My Father will love him, and we will come to him and make our home with him."*

Imagine that. The Creator of the whole universe wants to disclose himself to us, to make his home with us. And how does God do that? He does it through *all* the means of his grace, including scripture, sacrament, community, obedience, and service. But a crucial means, the most intimate means, is *prayer.*

On the night he was betrayed, while still in the upper room, Jesus offers his longest and most profound prayer. He opens it with these words:

> *Father, the hour has come. Glorify your Son, that your Son may glorify you. For you granted him authority over all people that he might give eternal life to all those you have given him. Now this is eternal life: that they know you, the only true God, and Jesus Christ, whom you have sent.* (John 17:1)

This is eternal life—*to know God.* It's a quality of life that begins now and survives beyond death. So if your prayers seem feeble to you right now, that's okay. *They're a start.* They put us on the road to a whole lot more—to knowing God himself.

And that's why we pray.

Chapter 2

Prayer in the Life of Christ

*But Jesus often withdrew to lonely
places and prayed.*
Luke 5:16

❧

In the first chapter we looked at the whole phenomenon of prayer in general. People pray—regardless of whether they claim to have a faith in God or not. It's a natural and unavoidable response to the presence of God that pervades our world on all levels, whether we acknowledge it or not. But just because we all pray doesn't mean that we pray *well*. Our prayers can actually become a dark and unhealthy response to the presence of God. Our prayers can be characterized by ignorance, superstition, manipulation, and idolatry. And so we need to step back and ask ourselves: What is *Christian* prayer?

Obviously, the best way to approach that question is to sit at the feet of Christ and learn what he thinks prayer really is. Which means we will be looking at some very familiar passages in the New Testament, but hopefully with fresh eyes. For starters, let's consider if and when Jesus prayed himself, beginning with some notable examples from the gospels:

- He was praying at his own baptism when the Spirit descended on him (Luke 3:21-22)).

- He spent an entire night alone in prayer prior to selecting the 12 apostles (Luke 6:12-16).

- He regularly went out to lonely places to pray alone (Luke 5:16, Matthew 14:23).

- He would get up early, while it was still dark, just to pray (Mark 1:35).

- He prayed prior to meals (Matthew 14:19, 15:36, 26:26).

- He prayed at the tomb of Lazarus prior to raising him from the dead (John 11:41-42).

- He prayed for the whole church in the upper room (John 17).

- He prayed during his agony in the garden at Gethsemane (Matthew 26:39-42).

- He prayed for his enemies (Luke 23:34).

- He prayed repeatedly to God during his suffering on the cross (Luke 23:46, Mark 15:34).

In short, Jesus prayed a lot. In Luke's gospel alone there are sixteen references to Jesus either praying or teaching on prayer. He prayed for a remarkably wide array of reasons and in virtually every kind of situation. He prayed publicly and privately, at the end of his sermons, while performing his miracles, or spontaneously for no apparent reason at all. He prayed short prayers and long ones. He prayed for his friends as well as his enemies. He prayed in joy and in suffering. He prayed with the agonized voice of Job and yet with the deep faith of someone who truly knew and trusted God. In other words, he prayed like someone for whom prayer was as natural and yet essential as breathing.

Which raises another question: If Jesus was "God's Son," and so powerful as to heal the sick, raise the dead, and calm the storm, why did he, of all people, have to pray so much? If Jesus is truly "God come in the flesh," then why would he even *need* to pray? This question requires that we think more deeply about Christ's incarnation. As Christians have confessed for twenty centuries, Jesus is both truly human and truly divine. Not simply God masquerading as a man, *nor* merely some man who became super-charged with God. Jesus is *both* truly God-in-the-flesh *and* truly human. And his humanity contained all the struggles and temptations of humanity in general. Consequently, Jesus prayed for the very same reasons we do.

Jesus tries to explain this reality in the fifth chapter of John's gospel. It's there we hear him claim that he is God's *unique* Son, and consequently he has the authority to give life and to judge all humanity. The Jewish rulers, understandably, accuse him of making himself equal to God, which from their perspective means he is claiming to be a rival god, and so they want

21

to kill him. Jesus' doesn't deny or minimize their assumption about his being equal to God, but rather he explains why he is not a *rival* god:

> *I tell you the truth, the Son can do nothing by himself; he can do only what he sees his Father doing, because whatever the Father does the Son also does. For the Father loves the Son and shows him all he does. ...By myself I can do nothing; I judge only as I hear, and my judgment is just, for I seek not to please myself but him who sent me.*

And how could Jesus know so perfectly what the Father is doing, and how does God so perfectly share with his Son his mind and will? Through prayer. In other words, Jesus prayed so much because *he had to*. Knowing and doing the will of God depended on it. The salvation of the world, you could say, depended on it. What's more, Jesus, in his incarnation, is our best and only true example of what *our* humanity was originally intended to look like—a living, breathing example of how life is meant to be lived and how it's sustained. And what we discover is that Jesus lived in constant and absolute dependence upon the Father. We see this most vividly when he prayed. Prayer was Jesus' lifeline to God. Without it he was at the mercy of the same destructive forces that each one of us know all too well.

What's more, prayer was a manifestation of his intrinsic trinitarian relationship with God. In his great prayer in John 17, Jesus reveals how important this unity was when he prays, *"Father, glorify your Son with the glory I had with you before the world began."* This was the end-game for Jesus, to be fully united with God. In a similar way, prayer becomes for us the means whereby we, too, sustain our connection to God.

But let's move from what we can observe from Jesus' life to what he actually taught. And there's no better place to begin than the *Sermon on the Mount* in Matthew's gospel. Well into the sermon we see Jesus zeroing in on various religious practices of his day. He gives us three common examples—charitable giving, fasting, and prayer. In each case he finds a similar problem with how these things were practiced. Listen to what he says about prayer:

> *And when you pray, do not be like the hypocrites, for they love to pray standing in the synagogues and on the street corners to be seen by men. I tell you the truth, they have received their reward in full. But when you pray, go into your room, close the door and pray to your Father, who is unseen. Then your father, who sees what is done in secret, will reward you.* (Matthew 6:5-6)

There are a lot of people who are big on prayer, but who are (according to Jesus) hypocritical in how they do it. They see prayer as an end in itself—a badge of spirituality—and that the mere practice of it somehow pleases God. So when Jesus describes someone standing on the street corner praying, we tend to see some kind of brazen, comical, cardboard hypocrite. But Jesus saw someone who, on the surface, would appear to be deeply pious, spiritual, and even admirable. But he also knew that much of this prayer was false precisely because of what was lacking on the inside.

But his teaching here prompts a question. Jesus instructs us to pray "in secret." When we earlier looked at how Jesus prayed, it wasn't always in secret. In fact, it was often very public. If it wasn't always in secret, then what is he actually teaching here? The crucial phrase in this whole passage is: *"pray to your Father."* The key to understanding Jesus' point is not so much always going into a private room and closing the door (although that can certainly be helpful), but rather making sure that our prayers are truly between God and us, and no one else. We pray to a Father who sees what's going on inside of us.

Dietrich Bonhoeffer, the famous German pastor and theologian, wrote a book entitled *The Cost of Discipleship*. In a passage on prayer, he writes that sometimes, even in our private rooms, we might as well be standing on a street corner, because we are still praying to someone other than God. We are praying to ourselves. We are watching ourselves pray and feeling good about satisfying some expected behavior that we think pleases God. This is not prayer, says Jesus. This is hypocrisy. Authentic prayer is a communication between *persons*; it is part of that personal relationship between us and God that I wrote about in Chapter 1. And consequently, it can happen anywhere, public or private. The private room is merely Jesus' common method of using contrasting language. It's his way of saying, "Take whatever steps necessary to ensure that your prayer is solely between you and God."

Which leads me to ask: Can you think of a time when you were in a group setting, and someone was leading the group in prayer, but it didn't feel like prayer at all? If you have experienced this, you are not alone. In our corporate prayers, it's very common for the person praying to go through the expected motions, maintain the proper image, and yet not be praying to God at all. It may be they are using prayer as a platform to make a point about something. I think this happens quite often, and every one of us is probably guilty of doing it.

Too often we use corporate prayer to lecture or cajole or preach or share lofty ideas and so forth, but it doesn't actually lead us into the presence of God. But the opposite can also happen in corporate prayer. Have you ever participated in a group prayer that actually drew you into to the presence of God? I certainly have. In fact, I've been part of group prayer where my mind and spirit were distracted or bothered about other things, and yet the minute the prayer began, the person doing the praying pulled me with them into the presence of God. This is the gift of people who understand and practice genuine prayer.

But let's continue to listen to Jesus from the *Sermon on the Mount*:

And when you pray, do not keep on babbling like pagans, for they think they will be heard because of their many words. Do not be like them, for your father knows what you need before you ask him. (Matthew 6:7-8)

What is going on here? Is Jesus saying that all prayer should be brief? Were all of Jesus' prayers brief? No, for the entire 17th chapter of John is one continuous prayer. Most of Jesus' prayers were brief, but not always. The key to understanding this passage is to ask yourself: In religions that encourage prayers of endless repetition—for example, prayer wheels or mantras or whatever—what does such a practice assume about their god or the purpose of prayer? It assumes that the deity is either reluctant to respond or desirous of prayers that go on for a long time. By way of contrast, how does Jesus describe God? He tells us repeatedly that our Father is eager to respond and does so with our very best at heart. Indeed, as he tells us, God knows what we are going to say even before we say it!

But are non-Christians the only ones who babble on in their prayers? No, we Christians fall prey to this also. Unfortunately, there is a whole theology of prayer that advocates a certain kind of persistence in prayer that's supposed to insure we receive what we are asking for. By failing to really understand two specific texts in Luke's gospel, a lot of Christians believe either that God can be worn down through constant prayer, or that God evaluates the sincerity of our prayers by how long and often we ask them. Some Christians call this "storming heaven," as if God will not respond unless we demonstrate such persistence. It's a tragic and ultimately dishonoring view of God.

The first text they appeal to is in Luke 18. The chapter opens with a parable that specifically describes a persistent request that gets answered:

> *Then Jesus told his disciples a parable to show them that they should always pray and not give up. He said, "In a certain town there was a judge who neither feared God nor cared about men. And there was a widow in that town who kept coming to him with the plea, 'Grant me justice against my adversary.' For some time he refused, but finally he said to himself, 'Even thought I don't fear God or care about men, yet*

because this widow keeps bothering me, I will see that she gets justice, so that she won't eventually wear me out with her coming!" (Luke 18:1-5)

This certainly sounds like a lesson in badgering God, but in what follows, Jesus teaches the exact opposite:

Listen to what the unjust judge says. And will not God bring about justice for his chosen ones, who cry out to him day and night? Will he keep putting them off? I tell you, he will see that they get justice, and quickly. However, when the Son of Man comes, will he find faith on the earth? (Luke 18:6-8)

In other words, is the unjust judge in the parable supposed to represent God? No! Jesus meant for him to be the antithesis to God. The parable is a picture of how things get done in the world, but *not* how things get done with God. Jesus is specifically saying that we can leave our burdens with God, knowing that he will answer us "quickly." This also helps us understand the words that open the chapter: *"Then Jesus told his disciples a parable to show them that they should always pray and not give up."* Jesus is trying to encourage prayer *in general* by letting us know how responsive God is to our prayers, not that he is unresponsive and needs cajoling.

We shouldn't pray in order to get from God what he doesn't already want to give us. Rather we should pray so that we might draw near to him, to share our burdens, to learn more of who he is and to remember *that he knows what we need even before we even ask him.* The real question, as Jesus points out at the end of the passage, is whether we trust God. Do we want what God wants? *"When the Son of Man comes, will he find faith*

27

on the earth?" And to ensure that our faith stays strong, Jesus tells us to be *always* praying in general and not to become discouraged. Open your heart to God. Share your mind. Learn to listen. But he is *not* teaching that we need to badger God or keep repeating the same request over and over in hopes that things will change. He is teaching that we should trust that God hears and answers our prayers.

The second passage that people use to justify a false kind of persistence in prayer is found in Luke 11:1-13. It opens with Jesus' disciples observing what a huge role prayer played in Jesus' life, and so they come to him seeking guidance:

> *One day Jesus was praying in a certain place. When he finished, one of his disciples said to him, "Lord, teach us to pray, just as John taught his disciples."*

In response Jesus gives a shorter version of the Lord's Prayer and quickly follows it with a parable to encourage them to keep praying, since it often seems in our experience that our prayers have little effect. Think about our own lives. After praying the Lord's Prayer in the morning, how many of us, at the end of the day, can honestly claim that we have fully honored the name of God and accomplished his will? How many of us can claim we have been fully content with our daily bread and didn't grumble at all? Or how aware have we been of our own sins committed, and what's more, how truly repentant have we been? And how forgiving have we been to those who may have sinned against us? And how did we handle the day's normal barrage of temptations?

And so in Luke 11 he follows the Lord's Prayer

with this parable:

> *Suppose one of you has a friend, and he goes to him at midnight and says, 'Friend, lend me three loaves of bread, because a friend of mine on a journey has come to me, and I have nothing to set before him.' Then the one inside answers, 'Don't bother me. The door is already locked, and my children are in bed. I can't get up and give you anything.' I tell you, though he will not get up and give him the bread because he is his friend, yet because of the man's boldness he will get up and give him as much as he needs.*

The word translated "boldness" here is a difficult word. This is the only place in the New Testament it is used. In the Greek literature of the day it meant literally "shamelessness." In subsequent centuries it took on the added meaning of "persistence," and many people since have taken this parable (like the parable in Luke 18) to mean that it's a sign of effective prayer to keep asking God for something until you get it. Once again, Jesus is actually teaching the opposite. But let's review the parable itself.

In hearing this story, we often side with the man who needs the bread and we are somewhat appalled by his supposed friend who seems so uncaring. But listen again to the details. The first man has company that shows up at midnight. Since there was no such thing as refrigeration in Jesus' day, bread was baked daily and usually just enough for the day. We often hear about how important hospitality was (and still is) in middle-eastern cultures, and this is true, but no one, in any culture, arriving at a friend's home at *midnight*, would expect their host to go running through the neighborhood to wake people up in order to feed them. This was, indeed, a bold and even shameless thing to do.

What is more, most homes were often very small, with only one bedroom where whole families slept together. There was no central heating, and so they would often sleep together in order to share body heat. It's midnight, there is this knocking at the door, and the man in bed knows that to get up would likely mean waking his entire family. Plus the whole request is ridiculous in the first place. *Wait until morning and then ask! Your company can wait! Just who do you think you are?* And yet…and yet, Jesus is right. While he won't get up for friendship or social protocol or because it's a reasonable request, yet his friend's over-the-top, shocking and shameless effort leaves him no choice but to give him what he needs in order to pacify him. This parable is at once funny, ridiculous, and absurd.

And it begs the same question as the parable in Luke 18: Is God like the man in bed? Of course not! Just as in Luke 18, where God is not the unjust judge, so here God is the complete opposite of the man in bed. He *wants* to respond to our entreaties. The problem is never God's indifference or reluctance or inability, *but our unbelief.* We lack the boldness of the man in need of bread to even ask. Sometimes we don't pray because our problems seem so immense and insoluble that we don't really believe God can do anything about it. Then again, our problems may seem too petty. At other times it's our own unworthiness that gets in the way. We are like the double-minded man that James talks about in his epistle (1:5-7). This is why Jesus quickly follows the parable with these words of encouragement beginning in verse nine:

*So I say to you: Ask and it will be given to you; seek
and you will find; knock and the door will be opened
to you. For everyone who asks receives; he who seeks
finds, and to him who knocks, the door will be opened.
Which of you fathers, if your son asks for a fish, will
give him a snake instead? Or if he asks for an egg,
will give him a scorpion? If you then, though you are
evil, know how to give good gifts to your children, how
much more will your Father in heaven give the Holy
Spirit to those who ask him?*

If we sinful people know how to treat those we
love, how much more does God? But there is one last
clue in verse 13 that transforms this whole passage on
prayer that I don't want you to miss. Life is difficult
and our struggles are often complex. Often we have a
specific thing we need—a job, a friend, better health.
Sometimes we need understanding, discernment or
wisdom. Sometimes we need direction or comfort.
When Jesus says to ask, seek, knock, he is using
language that tries to capture the whole gamut of what
prayer involves. Prayer involves all of life.

But there have always been those who have taught
that as we move into the higher spheres of spirituality
that we cease to use prayer as a way of asking for
"things" and enter into some kind of pure, mystic
contemplation of God. This is nonsense. If there is
one thing that characterized how Jesus prayed, whether
he was seeking guidance prior to choosing the twelve
apostles or agonizing in the garden of Gethsemane, it's
that prayer always includes our immediate needs—
whether material, emotional, or spiritual.

But as we listen to this passage and come to verse
13, the reader expects to hear Jesus say, "If you then,

though you are evil, know how to give good *gifts* to your children, how much more will your Father in heaven give good *gifts* to those who ask him!" (which is how Matthew's gospel actually records the same statement). But instead of using the word "gifts" at the end, Luke substitutes "the Holy Spirit," which to the sensitive reader sounds at first like a *non sequitur*. And yet it is entirely in keeping with the overriding concern of what Jesus is saying about prayer.

In the end, what God is doing in our prayers is not merely meeting our needs but giving us *himself* through the Holy Spirit. The Holy Spirit is not merely the One who brings various gifts to the Church, but he is himself (as St. Paul tells us) the seed of God's own life that comes into us as we seek God. As we grow in prayer over a lifetime, we discover that God does more than simply hear us. He comes to us. Yes, he answers our prayers, but even more importantly, God gives us himself.

Let's now return to our original passage in the *Sermon on the Mount* where Jesus was telling us not to babble repetitively like the pagans. There is a great passage in Ecclesiastes that I always think of whenever I read this advice on prayer. I can't help but wonder if it wasn't in Jesus' mind when he gave this teaching:

> *Guard your steps when you go to the house of God. Go near to listen rather than to offer the sacrifice of fools, who do not know that they do wrong. Do not be quick with your mouth, do not be hasty in your heart to utter anything before God. God is in heaven and you are on earth, so let your words be few. ...many words are meaningless. Therefore stand in awe of God.* (Ecclesiastes 5:1-2, 7)

There is an awesomeness about God that should always pervade our prayers. This is why, for thousands of years, Jews and Christians have found kneeling to be an instinctive posture in prayer. Not essential, but a natural response to a holy God. Yes, our approach to God should always be genuine, personal, and not "stained-glass" or artificial. But at the same time, it should never become casual or ordinary. In prayer we stand on holy ground.

In summary, short prayers can be just as meaningful and effective as long ones. But our prayers *can* be long—especially when we have an unusually heavy load or our situation is very complex. Sometimes it takes a fair number of words just to sort out what it is we are really praying for. But these kinds of prayers, where we are struggling to even articulate to God the deepest burdens of our heart, ought to be reserved for our private prayer and not inflicted on an entire group in corporate prayer! And even privately we need to always remember that as we pray, the Holy Spirit is there praying in and through us to God, as Paul reminds us in his epistle to the Romans (8:26-27):

> *In the same way, the Spirit helps us in our weakness. We do not know what we ought to pray for, but the Spirit himself intercedes for us through wordless groans. And he who searches our hearts knows the mind of the Spirit, because the Spirit intercedes for God's people in accordance with the will of God.*

Finally, returning to Jesus' teaching on prayer from the *Sermon on the Mount,* notice what he says after telling us not to babble in our prayers: "Your Father knows what you *need* before you ask him." Here Jesus reminds us that God meets our *needs* and not our *wants*.

This is very important. Remember the discussion in Chapter 1 regarding Peter's reaction to Jesus after that miraculous catch of fish, when he falls to his knees and begs Jesus to go away and leave him alone. This recognition of his own sinfulness and this desire to be as far away from Jesus as possible was a very real *want* on Peter's part at that point. Fortunately, Jesus totally disregards the request. Instead he saw into his heart and understood that this desire was a result of Peter's *need* for forgiveness and healing. And so Jesus met his need and not his want.

But if God knows the need even before we ask, then obviously our prayers in no way "inform" God of anything. I realize I shouldn't have to point this out, but I think we all need to be reminded of this from time to time. When I listen to some people pray, it's as if God needed to be brought up to speed on what needs to happen. They give God an outline of what he needs to do, rather than simply tell him their burden.

But that provokes another question: If God knows our true needs already, then why pray at all? The answer to that common question should now be clear. We pray because, like Jesus himself, we need to. We have no other place to go, no other place to lay down our burdens and know they are being addressed. If, as we learned in Chapter 1, becoming connected to God is the whole point of our existence and the deepest ache of our hearts, and prayer is a crucial means to actually connecting with God, then regardless of the fact that God already knows what I am about to ask for or regardless of whether I finally get what I feel I need from God, *I am going to pray,* for God alone fully understands my situation and is capable of bringing resolution. We lay our burdens down before God because we have no other place to leave them, no other person who can ultimately deal with all the complexities of our lives. We pray because we must, for we have nowhere else to go.

Imagine a high school quarterback losing the championship game in the waning seconds by fumbling the ball on the five-yard line. Obviously, when he goes to meet his girlfriend after the game, he is carrying a huge burden. If he is immature and their relationship is poor, he will be sullen or distant or even angry with her. If he is mature and they have a good relationship, he is going to share his pain with her in agonizing detail (much like King David does in the Psalms). Yes, he knows she was actually sitting in the front row and already knows all about it. And yes, he knows she would do anything in her power to get him through this. But he will share the burden with her just the same, because in the sharing of the burden, the load itself becomes more tolerable. Their relationship becomes stronger, more transparent, more intimate. Isn't that what we want with our relationship with God?

Now the weakness of this example is that there is little his girlfriend can do but be a good listener. God, however, is infinitely powerful, and he has already been at work in that whole scenario even before the football game began, working to build and shape that young man. And so, in prayer, I not only lay all my burdens and pain down before the Lord, but I have the assurance that God is already at work in that very situation. In prayer I am actually meeting with my Creator, my Father, my Savior, my Lord, and everything else that an encounter with God involves. Yes, in disclosing my true self, I will be sharing an awful lot of burdens that I would like God to address. Yes, I know he already knows all about these things. And yes, I know that God will do the right thing regardless of what I say. But I bring them to him anyway, because I have no other place to go, no one else who can help in the manner he can.

Which means, when Jesus teaches us how to pray, he is actually teaching us how to live. The whole attitude of prayer (the authentic, true me living *transparently* and *dependently* with God), this is the stuff that defines the Christian life.

Now the topic of prayer concludes in the *Sermon on the Mount* with the Lord's Prayer, which I am going to save for the next chapter. Many people know it by heart, but we still need to ask ourselves: Why did Jesus give us this prayer, and by doing so, what is he saying about prayer in general?

Chapter 3

The Lord's Prayer

At that time Jesus said, "I praise you,
Father, Lord of heaven and earth, because
you have hidden these things from the
wise and the learned, and revealed them
to little children."
Matthew 11:25

&⊸⤳

As we continue to listen to Jesus' specific teaching on prayer, I have intentionally left the Lord's Prayer as a separate topic. Many of the major Christian denominations dedicate a lot space to the Lord's Prayer in their respective catechisms. Many Christians (as well as non-Christians) know it by heart and may already use it. At the end of the last chapter, I asked readers to think about two questions in regards to the Lord's Prayer: Why did Jesus give us this prayer, and what does it say about prayer in general?

Why did Jesus give us this prayer? Another way to approach this question is to ask: Did Jesus give us a "prescribed" prayer—a prayer that should be repeated word for word—or did he give us a model of what is involved in prayer? It would seem from the prayers of Jesus himself that he largely intended the Lord's Prayer as an example of what ought to be the *focus* of our prayers, and not so much as a prayer to be merely repeated.

But does that mean that repeating the Lord's Prayer has no value? Of course not. Christians of all persuasions—Catholic, Orthodox, Protestant—recite the Lord's Prayer on specific occasions and this can have great value. There are times in my own private prayer when I simply get stuck. Reciting the Lord's Prayer can often put me back on track as to what prayer is all about. But it can do that because I have meditated long and hard on that second question: What does the Lord's Prayer say about prayer in general? To answer this question, we need to take some time to reflect on it in more detail. It begins:

- "*Our* Father…" By beginning with "our" Father and not "my" Father, what does this prayer do to us? This opening word challenges our ego-centric spirituality right at the start. God is not our private domain, nor is our pursuit of God entirely a solo journey. Throughout the gospels, Jesus lays great stress on the fact that we are part of a larger community of believers and that our spiritual health and growth depends on our being connected to other believers. We are always praying *with* believers all over the world, which is why our corporate prayers are just as important as our private prayers.

- "Our *Father*..." Why this name for God? Our entire Christian life (including prayer) is about building a relationship with a Living God who longs to draw close to us as a father. And although each of us bring different connotations to the word "father," what specifically might Jesus have wanted to convey? The opening of John's gospel captures it well: "But as many as received him [Jesus]...he gave the right to become children of God—children born not of natural descent, nor of human decision or a husband's will, but born of God." He not only created us physically, but those who turn to God in repentance and faith are reborn by his Holy Spirit into something entirely new—a living, spiritual connection with God in which his life is shaping us into changed beings. He becomes our source of wisdom, guidance, and *life*.

- "...who art in heaven..." What does this phrase add? Even as our Father, God remains transcendent and beyond our complete understanding. We must never lose sight of this, no matter how close we may come to God. There should always be a holy and reverent awe of God. In fact, as we draw closer to him in genuine prayer, there should grow a growing awareness of just how holy and glorious he truly is. In our corporate prayers, I am sometimes shocked to hear people talk to God as if he were a fishing buddy or something.

- "...hallowed be your name." It's not enough to recognize God's holiness as a concept or as an emotional reaction. Here we are praying that his holiness become a reality in my life (that is, in how I actually think and live) and in the world around me. I am asking God that in my thoughts, words, and deeds, may everything I do bring glory to his name. And by "name," Jesus is employing a semitic idiom. One's name represented the whole person. To tarnish a name is to tarnish the whole person.

- "Your kingdom come, your will be done, on earth as it is in heaven." Here we are asking that God's rule would fully come to this broken world, beginning with my own life. It is both a prayer for the future and a submission to God in the present. In a very real sense, this phrase is the practical explanation for what it means to "hallow God's name." Our prayers should always be grounded in this very basic desire—to know and do God's will. Too often we pray this with resignation—"Lord, help me to accept your will"—rather than with an eager desire. If we discover that we are praying with resignation, then we have something additional to pray for—a changed heart.

- "Give us this day our daily bread." How has the overall prayer now shifted? It's now focusing on our practical needs, and yet seeking only enough for today. It's very restricted and humble. It isn't focused on what may happen tomorrow. And what does that say about God? It is a prayer of faith that assumes God is in control of tomorrow. Or as Jesus put it, *"Therefore do not worry about tomorrow, for tomorrow will worry about itself. Each day has enough trouble of its own"* (Matthew 6:14).

- "And forgive us our sins as we forgive those who sin against us." It's easy to understand why in our prayers we seek forgiveness for wrongs we've done, but why does Jesus make this connection between what we do wrong and the wrongs others do to us? When we seek forgiveness from God, we are doing several things at once. First, we are acknowledging that it is God who we have injured. If this wasn't so, we would only ask forgiveness from those we injured. But we know that ultimately the one who has been violated the most is God himself. Second, we are also asking God to do something we don't really deserve or merit. We want him to forgive us out of his sheer mercy and grace. We can never undo all the harm we've caused, and so we come to God and simply throw ourselves on his mercy. But if we turn around and don't extend that same mercy to those who have injured us, what does that say about our *true* belief in how life ought to be lived? It says that deep down inside we actually believe that those who hurt people should be punished for their sins. And if that's what we really believe, Jesus says, that's precisely how God will treat our sins. Not a happy thought! In fact, after giving us the Lord's Prayer, Jesus tacks on a warning: *"If you do not forgive those who sin against you, neither will your Father in heaven forgive you of your sins."*

- "And lead us not into temptation, but deliver us from evil." The apostle James tells us that God will never tempt us to *do* evil, so what are we praying for here? Are we asking God to spare us from all temptation? Wasn't Jesus himself lead by the Holy Spirit into the wilderness to be tempted by the devil? This specific request is an idiomatic way of saying "don't let sin get the upper hand over me." God is more than willing to allow us to undergo temptation (although his intentions are always to build us up and not cause us to sin), but he is also readily available to help us endure the test and to overcome evil. This is what we are praying for here. But as Jesus tells us in Matthew 18:7, "it is necessary that temptations come."

The Lord's Prayer actually ends here. In the old King James Bible, we have the famous doxology at the end of the prayer: "For thine is the kingdom, the power and the glory forever, amen." In virtually all of our modern translation, that verse is omitted. When the King James version translated the Greek into English, the scholars had only a half dozen ancient manuscripts to work from, the oldest of which dated from around the 11th century. With the advent of archeology, we now have over 5,000 full or partial manuscripts and papyri of the New Testament, the oldest of which (fragments of John's gospel) have been carbon dated back to around 120 AD. So obviously our modern understanding of the original text is vastly superior. What appears to have happened is that by the second century the Lord's Prayer had become a fixed part of the church's liturgy, and like most liturgical prayers, a formal doxology was added in the margins of some manuscripts, which caused it to eventually enter the text itself. But it was certainly not part of the prayer Jesus gave us. Is it appropriate to recite it in public prayer? Sure! Why not? To pray "Thine is the kingdom and the power and the glory forever, amen" is a wonderful tribute to God.

And so, in summary, with very few words this prayer covers the broad sweep of our everyday life. Consequently, what happens to us when we meditate on and pray the Lord's Prayer over a long period of time? The form itself eventually dissolves and what is left is an orientation, an outlook, a sensibility for what all real prayer is about. For in the Lord's prayer, God is at the center of everything. There is praise, repentance, and recognition of our total dependence on him. Even when we ask for things, such as our daily bread, it is a very restricted and carefully defined request. It's not for bigger barns or enough investments so we never have to worry (or pray) again. It is for just enough to get us through today, which means it's a prayer that recognizes how much we lean on God for our existence every moment of the day. And should God someday take away even our daily bread, we are not deterred from trusting him, for we have already asked that his will be done.

Because Jesus gives us this as a "model" prayer, it is often used in public worship, which seems very appropriate to me. We will consider the value of liturgical prayer in the next chapter, but let it be said here that just as the Lord's Prayer can shape our individual personal prayers, so it has historically shaped the worship of Christian communities around the world.

One way of using this prayer that's helped me a great deal involves praying it one word or phrase at a time. For example, years ago I was on vacation for several weeks and would rise while it was still dark and just sit on the porch and watch the sunrise. During this time I would take one word or phrase and just pray it to God, meditating on what it meant in general as well as what it meant for me on that particular day. But the variety of ways this prayer can aid us are too numerous to mention.

There is one final passage where Jesus explicitly teaches about prayer that I want to explore. In addition to the *Sermon on the Mount*, as well as Luke 11 and 18, prayer is mentioned frequently in the longest discourse given by Christ in the New Testament (in John 13-17, often called the *Upper Room Discourse*). These five chapters take place on the night he was betrayed into the hands of his enemies. He is preparing his closest disciples for what lies ahead, as well as teaching them about something extraordinary that is coming after his resurrection. With the coming of the Holy Spirit *into* the life of believers, both the Father and the Son will likewise become more present to them.

> *"On that day you will realize that I am in my Father, and you are in me and I am in you. Whoever has my commands and obeys them, he is the one who loves me. He who loves me will be loved by my Father, and I too will love him and show myself to him. …If anyone loves me, he will obey my teaching. My father will love him, and we will come to him and make our home with him."* (John 14:20-21, 24)

And because of this reality, prayer itself becomes all the more essential, for it is the means whereby we connect to this reality. Three times during this long discourse, Jesus encourages his disciples to pray (14:12-14, 15:7-8, and 16:22-26). Unfortunately, there is a statement in each of these three texts that has been taken out of context and used to promote a very wrong assumption about prayer. The phrases taken from each text are as follows:

- 14:14 – *"You may ask me for anything in my name, and I will do it."*
- 15:7 – *"...ask whatever you wish, and it will be given you."*
- 16:23 – *"...my Father will give you whatever you ask in my name."*

There is an entire history of bad consequences that has come from taking these statements out of their individual contexts. There's no end of writers and preachers who have taught that if we only believed hard enough or sincerely enough, then God will give us whatever we want, whether it's more money in the bank or the healing of a crippled son or daughter. How many times have we read in the newspapers of a child dying for want of medical care because the parents were told they shouldn't rely on medicine but rather "look to God in prayer"?

What is remarkable is that when these verses are read *in* context, they are all promising us something entirely different. In John fourteen Jesus tells his disciples that they will not only continue his ministry, but they will have an even greater impact since in his resurrection Jesus would be available to them in a universal and more powerful way, since, as he puts it, *"I am going to the Father."* It is immediately after promising this that he tells them, *"You may ask me for anything in my name, and I will do it."* Because he's promising to continue his ministry through us, it means we will be praying for things related to that ministry. We will be praying for open doors, receptive hearts, wisdom in how we share the gospel, protection from those who would subvert the message of Christ.

In the passage from John fifteen something similar is happening. This chapter opens with that well know metaphor of Christ as the vine and his followers as branches, a people who are completely dependent on his indwelling life as their means of becoming "fruitful." Bearing fruit becomes a big theme in this passage as the primary evidence of genuine faith—the fruit of Christ's Spirit in our own life and in the impact we have on others. And so the context reads: *"If you remain in me* [as a branch in a vine] *and my words remain in you, ask whatever you wish, and it will be given you. This is my Father's glory, that you bear much fruit, showing yourselves to be my disciples."* So what is the whole point of this text? That we bear fruit to God's glory. And what two things does he mention that aid us in this? (1) Making sure his words remain in us, and (2) praying continually so that this intimate connection with the vine is maintained. So what will we be praying for? More money? Miraculous things? Or for wisdom in understanding his word and the grace to obey it (and thereby "bearing fruit")?

Or take the third example from John sixteen. In this passage Jesus is acknowledging the very real grief the disciples are experiencing at the prospect of his imminent departure. He tells them in verse 20: *"I tell you the truth, you will weep and mourn while the world rejoices. You will grieve, but your grief will turn to joy."* Then he says again in verse 22: *"Now is your time of grief, but I will see you again and you will rejoice, and no one will take away your joy."* Jesus is describing the radical transformation that would overtake these disciples when they witnessed the resurrected Christ. And part of that transformation will be their understanding that in and through Christ they can now approach God the Father in prayer with a boldness and immediacy they never knew before, and so in the very next verse he adds: *"In that day you will no longer ask me anything. I tell you the truth, my Father will give you whatever you ask in my name. Until now you have not asked for anything in my name. Ask and you will receive, and your joy will be complete."* And to reinforce this new link to God, he adds in verse 26: *"In that day you will ask in my name. I am not saying that I will ask the Father on your behalf. No, the Father himself loves you because you have loved me and believed that I came from God."*

The whole point of this passage in John 16 is that with the death and resurrection of Christ we have a new and open access to God. Our sins have been forgiven, our estrangement from God has been healed, and we can now approach God as his own beloved children. We pray "in Jesus' name," since it is through his atoning sacrifice that this new access is even possible, but we pray primarily to the Father. And like all good and loving fathers, God longs to give us what we *need* (although not always what we *want*, as we have already observed). This is the promise of these verses, that God is *always* attentive to our prayers, *always* answers them according to his wise and discerning love.

In John's first epistle, he summarizes all of this by writing:

> *This is the confidence we have in approaching God: that if we ask anything according to his will, he hears us. And if we know that he hears us—whatever we ask—we know that we have received what we asked of him.* (I John 5:14-15)

Please note that key phrase, *"according to his will."* That is how we are to pray. Even in our most desperate prayers, even when we feel that what we are asking for is a just and good and necessary thing, *even then* we have to allow God to be God and answer our prayers according to his wise and (at times) incomprehensible will.

But regardless of the outcome, God *does* answer prayer. Always. We may not see it or understand it. The pain that prompted us to pray in the first place may stay with us for a very long time. But as we draw near to God in prayer something else happens. What Jesus promised in John 14:21 increasingly becomes a reality: *"He who loves me will be loved by my Father, and I too will love him and show myself to him."* As we become more acquainted with the Father and the Son, as we are drawn closer to God and allow him to "show" himself to us, we learn to trust him and to rest in his sovereign care. We discover that he truly does know what he is doing, and for those who discover this, their prayers are *always* answered.

Chapter 4

Learning to Pray

Rejoice in your hope, be patient in difficulties,
be constant in prayer.
Romans 12:12

$\approx\ll$

By way of review, in Chapter 1 we asked, "What is prayer, and why do people pray?" Then in the next two chapters we essentially asked, "What is Christian prayer?" And we tried to answer that by simply looking at the life and teaching of Jesus regarding prayer. What we learned was that prayer for him was as natural and essential as breathing, and that prayer was his lifeline to God—the means by which he maintained his deep communion and unity with the Father. And so it must be for us.

We then went on to hear him give us some basic parameters to our prayers. First, genuine prayer is solely between us and God. Even our corporate prayers ought to be solely between all of us together and God. Second, God is always eager to hear and respond to our prayers, even when he seems distant or silent, and thus we don't have to employ a lot of unnecessary words in order to be heard. Like Jesus himself, our prayers can be simple, direct, and heartfelt. Third, God knows what we need, even before we ask, and thus prayer is not about informing God about things, but about laying our burdens down before him. The essence of prayer is learning how to be totally "naked" before God, allowing the real me to share from my heart what is going on—whether that be joy, sorrow, gratitude, confusion, and even unbelief. Jesus' prayers in the gospel cover a huge variety of human situations and emotions, and we ought to do likewise.

In that parable from Luke 11, we saw how "shameless" prayer can be, that nothing is off limits, that God is always available and eager to respond. Which is why after giving us the parable, Jesus closes his teaching on prayer by telling us that if we "ask, seek, knock," we *will* receive an answer. But such an admonition also assumes that we have the humility, faith, and patience to listen and to be taught. In short, in teaching us how to pray, Jesus is actually teaching us how to live—how to live a life that is wholly dependent on God every moment of every day—seeking his will, pleasure, guidance and strength. Finally, we learned from Jesus that prayer is ultimately about developing a relationship with the living God, which means learning how to listen as well as how to speak.

And so now I want us to become very practical and ask the question, "How do we foster healthier prayer in our individual lives, as well as with our corporate prayer?" I would like to start by making the observation that the health of our corporate prayer is built on the health of our individual prayer. People who seldom pray alone but still attend church will find corporate pray to be largely formulaic, ritualistic and even empty. They may appreciate corporate prayer on a superficial level, especially when the person praying is eloquent or emotional, but seldom will it personally connect them to God in a lasting, meaningful way. And the reason for this is that they themselves don't know what real prayer is like. Even if everyone around them is deeply involved in the prayer, they will remain outsiders to what is actually going on.

So to get practical, we have to start with our own individual prayer. And the most basic, obvious, and yet difficult starting point is the need to set aside times to pray regularly. That should be obvious, right? It's hard to grow in anything without being intentional and engaging in regular effort. Reading about prayer has very limited value (which is why I've tried to keep this book short). But *actually* praying can have immense value. And at the very least, I would suggest that once a day is needed for growing in prayer. Imagine a marriage that is on the rocks, and the marriage counselor asks the husband how often he has a significant conversation with his wife, and the man answers, "I make a point of having a deep conversation with her at least once a month." How adequate is that? Suppose the man tries to make amends by promising to have a significant conversation with his wife at least once a week—on Sundays. Is that really an improvement?

But in scheduling daily prayer, another hurdle emerges. We are now praying because we know we *ought* to. And what does that do to our prayer life? It kills it. Unless the motive in all our praying is a genuine hunger for God, to merely schedule prayer and dutifully do it will kill it. Unless we long to know, love, and serve God, our prayers will die.

But ironically, if you find yourself stuck in this place and lacking this essential motivation, then what can you do about it? You have a wonderful starting point for praying to God! You have a very genuine problem to bring to God. People who feel they lack the right motivation should begin their prayers with a very honest confession to God that God himself is not the deepest hunger of their life, and that they have a hard time sharing deeply with God. *If you ask God to change you in this, he will.* How he brings about this change may surprise you. It may require that God move in your life in ways that you would never have chosen but which drive you to pray nonetheless. It may even include some serious pain, or it may not. But if you honestly want to grow in prayer and you pray for that, God will make it happen.

But setting aside specific times to pray is only a start. As we grow in prayer—as it becomes more and more important to us—we find ourselves instinctively creating moments to pray throughout our day. We can be on the job and yet stop and breath a thank you, a praise, and a moment to just "center on God," which means remembering who he is, inviting him into whatever we are doing at that very moment. Some people even schedule these times on their cell phones. For many years I worked in the downtown core of a city and would walk to a Catholic church during my lunch hour to pray, since it was the only downtown church that was unlocked during the day.

Now, for those who are fairly new to prayer, setting aside time for extended prayer is fairly easy, but knowing what to do during this time can be hard. This is where some structure can help. For example, for thousands of years the Psalms in the Old Testament have been extremely helpful for many, many believers in learning how to pray. This ancient collection of 150 prayers have been used by Jews and Christians as a means of articulating prayer to God. For almost 40 years now I have been daily praying through one or two of the Psalms (starting with the first and just numerically going through them all). I learned this practice from the monks at a local Benedictine monastery. I don't study or analyze them, but pray them before God. And since they cover the whole range of human conditions, they invariably speak to where I am actually at. What's more, after praying a psalm or two, I find I can move more naturally into my own language with my own specific concerns.

For others, a liturgy of prayer can help, such as the "Daily Office" from the Book of Common Prayer, or some other formal structure. Personal prayer needs to become spontaneous to some degree in order to be genuine, but formal prayers can certainly help jump-start that process. The danger of any kind of structure, of course, is that we can be fooled into thinking that by the mere doing of the structure that we are praying. Whatever structure we use, we need to be vigilant that we remember the teaching of Christ—that all genuine prayer is "praying to the Father," actually sharing our real selves with the living God who sees our hearts— that we are not just going through the motions.

One of the first complaints I hear from those just

learning to pray is that their mind constantly wanders. Let it be said for the record that this is a problem for everyone! Some of us (and I am describing myself here) have minds that seem to know only one gear— hyper-drive—and thus the wandering-mind-syndrome is a constant challenge. But I have also learned some helpful wisdom from great saints of the past: when the mind begins to wander, don't become alarmed or try to shut the thought out. Just gently guide it to the exit door of your mind. You may have to do this repeatedly throughout your prayers, but these interruptions don't have to control your prayer.

Some other ways that might help you grow in prayer would include:

- Journaling: some people find it helps to write down what they are trying to articulate to God, or what they feel God is telling them. Over a long period, such journals can be immensely helpful in seeing trends or areas in our lives that God is working on, as well as our growing awareness of who God really is and what he wants to say to us.

- Meditation: this word has a broad range of meanings, some of which do not necessarily correspond to Christian prayer. But Christians have used the word for centuries to describe prayer as simply being in God's presence while we reflect on him, contemplating a particular aspect of his faithfulness, goodness, purity, wisdom, sovereignty, or love. Meditation moves us from thinking *about* God as an object or an abstraction and allows us to sit *with* him—in his very presence—becoming more and more aware of who he truly is.

56

- Walking: sometimes the biggest obstacle to focusing in prayer is that by sitting we become sleepy or distracted. Many people have discovered that a prayerful walk helps them stay more alert and focused.

- Reading theology, sermons, etc.: this sounds counter-intuitive, but for some people the bridge to prayer can often happen while we are engaged in spiritual reading of various kinds. A particular insight can suddenly bring God very near, causing us to stop and simply worship, give thanks, or lapse into a deep meditation of some kind.

- *Lectio divina*: this Latin phrase refers to a method of reading the scripture that originated in monasteries but is used around the world for hearing scripture within the framework of prayer. Different people use slightly different versions of *Lectio* (and the internet is a great resource in learning more), but essentially it involves reading a short passage of scripture and asking God to speak to you through that passage. It requires meditating on it *in the presence of God,* and then seeking to obey what you hear.

- There are likely a myriad of other approaches, postures, and helpful aids in prayer, but the key is to find what helps you given your own particular personality, situation in life, and circumstances.

Finally, I want to address the importance of learning to listen in prayer. This is at once both an essential part of prayer, but also the hardest thing for many people to understand and apply. It's also something that can most easily be abused. People can easily claim they have "heard" God telling them

something in prayer, when in actual fact they were
hearing their own thoughts and desires masquerading
as God's. Learning to hear God requires certain filters.
At a minimum, in order to hear God accurately, we
need to be:

- Deeply connected to Christ himself. For
  Christians, Christ is our window on God, and thus
  we need to know him intimately—who he is and
  what he taught—as well as practicing obedience to
  Christ in our daily lives. This requires that we are:

- Deeply connected to scripture. Our primary (and
  authoritative) knowledge of who Christ is and what
  he taught comes from the apostolic witness of the
  New Testament. To claim we have a word from
  Christ that contradicts scripture is certainly
  suspect. And to help us fully appreciate what we
  read in scripture, we should also be:

- Deeply connected to the teaching of Christians
  through the centuries. It's both presumptuous and
  dangerous to think that all by ourselves we can
  perfectly understand the scriptures. The basic
  message of the Bible is fairly clear, but as with
  anything, "the devil is in the details." We have
  twenty centuries of wonderful teachers if we are
  willing to be taught by them. And this means we
  must also be:

- Deeply rooted in a specific Christian community
  and allow mature Christians to have input into our
  life and hold us accountable for how we hear God.
  The most vulnerable Christian is the solo Christian
  who relies only on his or her own lights. And
  finally, all of this assumes that we are:

- Seriously engaged in obedience to all this input, that we are trying to live a life that pleases God through long practice. And a significant aspect of that obedience means we will be:
- Deeply involved in prayer.

Our "listening" to God needs to be filtered through all of the above. If what we hear in our prayers resonates with all of the above, then we ought to take it very seriously. Sometimes God actually calls us to a specific vocation, action, person in need, and so forth. Sometimes he wants to challenge us on how we spend our time or money or how we are relating to someone. Sometimes he wants to expand our understanding of how he is working in our lives and in the world. But in all of this, he wants to share *himself*—who he is, why we can trust him, and where he is taking us.

Next, I want to explore the value of corporate prayer. Trying to make group prayer meaningful has its own set of challenges. First, as I mentioned earlier, unless our personal prayer life is healthy, our corporate pray life with be largely "going through the motions." Unless we have learned how to stand before God as an individual—privately, transparently, and faithfully—it will be very difficult to do so in a group setting.

Historically, Christian churches have tended to utilize almost exclusively either liturgical or spontaneous group prayer (usually given by a single person). Both have value, but of the two the use of liturgical prayer over the centuries has had the greatest impact. And for good reason. In a letter written on April 1, 1952, C. S. Lewis makes an important point:

The advantage of a fixed form of service is

that we know what is coming. *Ex tempore* public prayer has this difficulty: we don't know whether we can mentally join in it until we've heard it—it might be phony or heretical. We are therefore called upon to carry on a critical and a devotional activity at the same moment: two things hardly compatible. In a fixed form we ought to have 'gone through the motions' before in our private prayers; the rigid form really sets our devotion *free*. I also find the more rigid it is, the easier it is to keep one's thoughts from straying. Also, it prevents getting too completely eaten up by whatever happens to be the preoccupation of the moment (i.e. war, an election, or what not). The *permanent* shape of Christianity shows through.

The beauty and depth of liturgical prayers that have been refined by Christians over hundreds of years can truly feed our souls. The challenge, of course, is to not engage in these prayers in a rote or unthinking manner. But if we have learned how to draw near to God in our private prayer, suddenly liturgical prayer takes on a whole new cast. We can more easily draw near to God together with all of those praying with us in a common voice. And it's our participation in this "common voice" that creates a kind of prayer that one person praying spontaneously for everyone doesn't.

This is not to say spontaneous prayer by a pastor or leader doesn't have value or cannot bring a group into the presence of God. The challenge here is that it takes people who are, in themselves, very mature in prayer to pull it off. A single person's spontaneous prayer too often wanders around and becomes unnecessarily long or tedious. Too often the person praying becomes preachy or emotional in an unhelpful way. And all it takes is for the person to utter something slightly political, obscure, or just plain wrong, and half the audience stumbles over it and becomes momentarily misdirected. By the time they can get into sync again, the prayer is over.

But spontaneous prayer can have an immediacy and power all its own, so I am not denying that it has an important place in a corporate setting. It just takes skill.

Chapter 5

Final Thoughts

For this is what the high and lofty One says—
he who lives forever, whose name is holy: "I live in
a high and holy place, but also with him who is
contrite and lowly in spirit, to revive the spirit of
the lowly and to revive the heart of the contrite."
Isaiah 57:15

❧

My youngest son attended college at Willamette University, in Oregon, studying environmental science. After his junior year he was given the dream summer job by the Department of Fish and Wildlife. His was to spend the summer driving to all the remote streams in the Coastal and Cascade Mountain ranges measuring the water flow in order to ensure that local farmers downstream didn't take too much water out and endanger the fish runs. The only problem was that his 1972 VW van wasn't very reliable and so he asked if he could use my truck for the summer. Now this was a truck I had really babied, but it was such a great opportunity, I couldn't say no.

Toward the end of the summer (and over 5,000 miles later), I was contacted by my son, who was calling from his cell phone. He had just survived a major accident on Highway 5 that was entirely his fault. He had merged onto the freeway too quickly and slammed into a very large flatbed truck, spun around 180 degrees right in the middle of traffic and then slammed into the cement wall along the medium strip. He was uninjured but my truck was banged up pretty badly. He was calling for help and advice, to apologize for what had happened, and to basically find a way to come to grips with his situation. He was obviously still shaken up a bit and talking rather randomly.

In an odd sort of way, he was just like any one of us when we pray to God.

I gave him what advice I could, but along the way I told him that the most important thing was that he wasn't hurt, and that I loved him. There was this very definite pause on the phone and suddenly the whole atmosphere changed. He replied in a very appreciative tone, "I know, Dad." And what had begun as a mere request for help had become—even if only for a short moment—the sharing of two hearts, two lives, two spirits.

In a very real sense, this is what can happen in prayer when we truly understand who we are praying to and what is happening between God and us. And yet, at the same time, I'm fully aware that this mundane, human analogy is *completely* inadequate when compared to the depth of what can actually happen when we come to God in prayer.

But there is one important caveat. The One who

made us and sustains us every moment of every day, who longs to meet us in prayer, will not force himself upon us, nor will he become less than who he actually is—the holy, sovereign, Lord of all, who is, at the same time, our loving Father. He invites us to pray, he continually seeks us out, but he requires that we respond just as earnestly.

Consequently, if you wait for the right setting, the right mood, the significant moment when you feel like you really have something to say to God, you will never learn to pray. It has to begin where you are at *right now*. So start where you are and begin the journey of prayer. Take small steps at first until you begin to find your stride. But whatever you do, don't give up. The "school of prayer" is in session for the whole of your life.

Speaking through the prophet Jeremiah (29:13), God declares, *"You will seek me and find me when you seek me with all your heart."* It is our heart that matters most to God. And if we honestly want to know him, he guarantees us that we will.

That's the one thing he *wants* us to pray for.

ABOUT THE AUTHOR

Mike Fargo spent most of his working career with the Internal Revenue Service as a Revenue Officer, Manager, and National Analyst. He is retired, and lives with his wife, Joy, in Oregon.

Made in the USA
Columbia, SC
13 February 2023

11922522R00045